Let Freedom Ring

Benjamin Franklin

by Susan R. Gregson

Consultant:
Roy E. Goodman, Curator of Printed Materials
American Philosophical Society Library
Philadelphia, Pennsylvania

Bridgestone Books
an imprint of Capstone Press
Mankato, Minnesota

Bridgestone Books are published by Capstone Press
151 Good Counsel Drive • P.O. Box 669 • Mankato, Minnesota 56002
http://www.capstone-press.com

Printed in the United States of America

Library of Congress Cataloging-in-Publication Data
Gregson, Susan R.
     Benjamin Franklin / by Susan R. Gregson.
          p.cm. — (Let freedom ring)
     Includes bibliographical references and index.
     ISBN 0-7368-1031-5
     1. Franklin, Benjamin, 1706–1790—Juvenile literature. 2. Statesmen—United States—Biography—Juvenile literature. 3. Inventors—United States—Biography—Juvenile literature. 4. Scientists—United States—Biography—Juvenile literature. 5. Printers—United States—Biography—Juvenile literature. [1. Franklin, Benjamin, 1706–1790. 2. Statesmen. 3. Printers. 4. Scientists.] I. Title. II. Series.
     E302.6.F8 G799 2002
     973.3´092—dc21   2001001144
                                                                                      CIP

Summary: A survey of the life of Benjamin Franklin, one of America's greatest inventors, philosophers, public servants, and political leaders. Follows Franklin's beginnings as a printer's apprentice, his life of public service and scientific experimentation, and his role as an originator and signer of the Declaration of Independence and other documents that created the United States of America.

Editorial Credits
Charles Pederson, editor; Kia Bielke, designer; Stacey Field, production designer; Deirdre Barton, photo researcher

Photo Credits
Stock Montage, cover, 21, 42 (top); Richard T. Nowitz/CORBIS, 5; Archive Photo, 6, 25; North Wind Picture Archive, 7, 9, 13, 31, 33, 34, 37, 42 (bottom); Capstone Press/Gary Sundermeyer, 10, 17; Hulton/Archive Photo, 16, 22, 27 (bottom); Andre Jenny/Unicorn Stock, 19; FPG International LLC, 23; Corbis, 27 (top); Art Resource/William James, 29; Photri-Microstock/Guilford Courth, 39; C P George/Visuals Unlimited, 41

2   3   4   5   6   07   06   05   04   03   02

Table of Contents

Chapter One

A Man of Many Talents

Imagine that it is 1788, and you are living in Philadelphia, Pennsylvania. A small gathering is to take place at your home. Food bubbles in the kettle in your kitchen fireplace. The room is warm, and good smells fill the air. You are waiting for a publisher, a writer, a scientist, an inventor, a philosopher, and a political leader.

You take a worried look around your tiny kitchen. How will you ever fit everyone around the table? Simple. Pull out a single chair and ask Benjamin Franklin to have a seat.

Ben was one of America's most brilliant men. He was a printer as a young man. After he sold his printing business, he spent years doing science experiments. You may remember the story about Ben flying a kite to discover electricity. Ben also invented many useful household items, all meant to ease daily life in colonial America.

Many people consider Benjamin Franklin to be one of America's most brilliant citizens.

Ben asked the French king for France's help in fighting the Revolutionary War. This was one way that Ben fought behind the scenes.

Ben had only two years of schooling when he was young. But colleges gave him honorary degrees for his science work as an adult.

Later in life, Ben became known for his negotiating skills. He helped people who disagreed solve their problems. When Britain and its American colonies disagreed on independence, however, Ben became a Patriot. He believed America should be independent of British rule.

During the Revolutionary War (1775–1783), Ben fought for America behind the scenes. He was every bit as important as General George Washington, who waged battles on the field. During and after the war, Ben was a respected political leader who helped shape America's future.

But Ben came from modest beginnings. Before he became a famous scientist and Patriot, he was the son of a maker of candles and soap.

Chapter Two

Young Ben

Ben was born in 1706 in a small house in Boston, Massachusetts. His family's long kitchen table was always crowded. Friendly arguments erupted, and Ben heard both sides of many issues. Young Ben soaked up information and asked many questions. Some nights, his father played merry fiddle tunes. Other evenings, Ben's uncle read his latest poem. At home, Ben probably learned most of the skills that served him well later in life.

Ben's father, Josiah Franklin, enrolled Ben in grammar school. Ben loved books and always read well, though he failed most of his math work. As an adult, he read many books on math and came to enjoy the subject very much.

Ben was in school for only two years because it was expensive. By age 10, he was working in Josiah's business. Ben boiled animal fat in large kettles to make candles and soap. He poured soap into large wooden molds and helped customers.

Ben was born in this simple house in Boston.

Try Making Soap

Colonial soap cleaned everything from floors to animals to people. Many people today make soap as a hobby. They use glycerin, a clear, odorless liquid. Here is an easy recipe for soap that you can make at home. Ask a parent, teacher, or other adult to help you.

What You Need

- Soap molds, milk cartons, or small cans
- Spray vegetable oil (unflavored)
- Glycerin soap base (unscented, clear)
- Chopping block
- Knife
- Glass measuring cup
- Microwave oven

- Potholder
- Soap coloring
- Toothpicks
- Waxed paper

Note: You can buy glycerin, coloring, and soap molds at hobby stores. You also can order soap-making supplies on the Internet.

Josiah Franklin's soap was made with a strong, burning acid called lye. Ben mixed the lye and animal fat during a long, hot, and sometimes dangerous process.

What You Do

1. Spray the molds with spray vegetable oil.

2. With a sharp knife, cut the glycerin into squares about the size of ice cubes.

3. Place cubes in a glass measuring cup and heat in microwave until melted (about one minute).

4. Using a potholder, pour the melted glycerin into a mold, carton, or can.

5. With a toothpick, swirl a drop of soap coloring into the melted glycerin.

6. Let soap cool for 30 minutes. Turn mold onto waxed paper to release soap. For milk carton mold, cut sides with scissors. For tin can, cut bottom with can opener and carefully push soap out.

7. Decorate your soap with paper, ribbon, or other items, if desired.

Ben and His Brother

When Ben turned 12 years old, Josiah apprenticed him to his half-brother James, a newspaper printer. Josiah thought Ben would be an excellent printer. Ben worked hard and quickly learned the printing business.

Apprentices

Children in the colonies became apprentices when they were about 12 to 14 years old. A family often signed a contract to pay the tradesman a monthly fee. The child usually lived with the tradesman and learned whatever the tradesman could teach.

An apprentice worked as long as 15 hours a day. After many years, the contract ended. By then, the apprentice knew enough to open his or her own shop.

Ben and James did not get along. James thought Ben was a know-it-all. Ben thought James was foolish for ignoring his ideas about running the shop.

Ben read as much as he could and also wrote articles about Boston events for James's newspaper. He knew James would not print something with Ben's name on it, so he signed the articles "Silence Dogood." Readers loved the articles, and James never knew who wrote them until Ben later told him.

Local leaders did not like some of the ideas James's newspaper printed. At one point, James was even sent to jail for the articles he printed. While he was gone, he needed Ben to run the shop. When his ill-tempered brother was released, Ben was

supposed to go back to being an apprentice. But
Ben did not want to take orders from his brother
any longer.

Ben Runs Away

At age 17, Ben ran away from his brother. James was
furious and made sure no other Boston printers
hired his younger brother.

One of Ben's jobs as an
apprentice was to carry
printer's type cases.
He later opened his
own printing shop as
a young man.

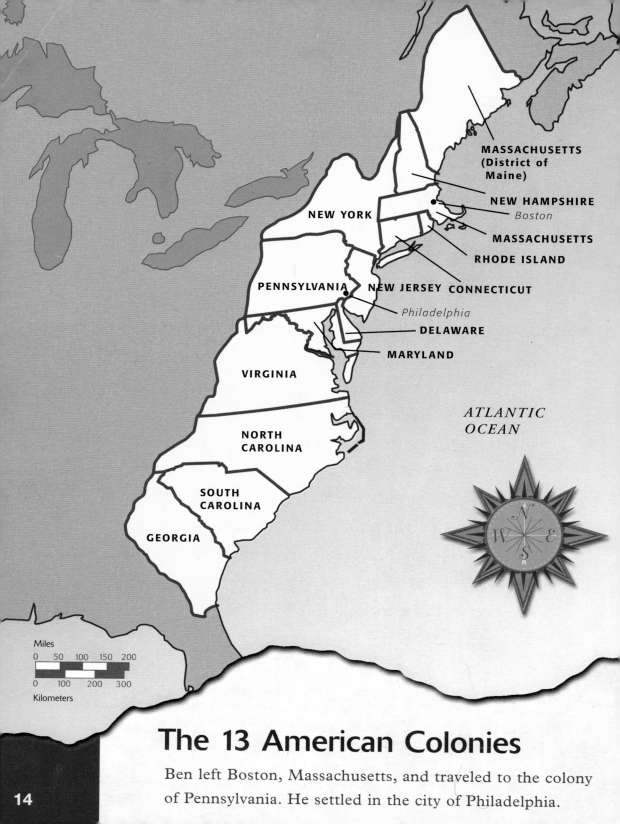

MASSACHUSETTS
(District of
Maine)

NEW HAMPSHIRE
Boston

MASSACHUSETTS

RHODE ISLAND

NEW YORK

PENNSYLVANIA

NEW JERSEY CONNECTICUT

Philadelphia

DELAWARE

MARYLAND

VIRGINIA

NORTH
CAROLINA

*ATLANTIC
OCEAN*

SOUTH
CAROLINA

GEORGIA

Miles
0   50   100   150   200

0   100   200   300
Kilometers

The 13 American Colonies

Ben left Boston, Massachusetts, and traveled to the colony
of Pennsylvania. He settled in the city of Philadelphia.

Ben left Boston and moved to Philadelphia, the capital of the Pennsylvania colony. In the 1700s, 13 British colonies hugged the Atlantic shore of North America. Among them were Massachusetts and Pennsylvania. Each colony had its own local government but was part of Britain. The British government made the laws that colonists lived by.

Ben arrived in Philadelphia with less than a dollar in his pocket. He soon found work with a Philadelphia printer. Within a year, Ben decided to start his own printing business.

Pennsylvania's governor, William Keith, encouraged Ben to set up a printing shop. He told Ben to go to Britain to buy the things he needed. The governor promised to send letters of credit so that Ben could get what he needed and pay for it later. But Keith never sent the letters, and Ben did not have enough money to sail home. He took work at a printer in London, the British capital.

In 1726, Ben returned to Philadelphia to work for the printer he had left two years earlier. Ben began to see a young woman named Deborah

The Printing Press

Colonial printing presses looked like a wooden table and frame. Type was handset in boxes called cases. The cases were inked by hand, then pressed against paper by tightening the huge screw with the handle.

Read Rogers. Her husband had gone to the West Indies, islands south of America, and was presumed dead.

Ben's Own Business

Ben did not get along well with his boss. By 1728, Ben had opened a shop with a friend. His former boss bought a newspaper called the *Pennsylvania Gazette* and tried to run Ben out of business.

However, Ben was an excellent printer and a smart businessman. After a year, Ben bought the *Gazette* from his old boss.

Ben wrote funny articles that poked fun at people and events. But he pretended that other people wrote them. Readers loved the articles, and his paper was a success.

In 1730, Ben married Deborah. From the print shop, she ran a general store that even included Josiah Franklin's soaps.

Ben brought a son, William, to the marriage. No one knows who William's mother was. Ben and William were close. In fact, a family friend described Ben as William's "friend, his brother, his intimate and easy companion."

After marriage, Ben and Deborah had two children, Francis and Sarah. "Frankie" died of a disease when he was only 4 years old. Sarah lived to take care of Ben in his old age. But in the 1730s, Ben's success was only beginning.

Chapter Three

Ben's Ideas

Ben loved Philadelphia and his new home. He published a lively newspaper. He even helped print Pennsylvania's money. Ben's family became a respected part of the community.

For more than 30 years, Ben and some friends met each week to talk about world events. Their name was the Leather Apron Club, since most of them were tradesmen who wore leather aprons. Members of the group often shared books. This gave Ben the idea to create colonial America's first public library in 1731.

"Poor Richard"

In 1732, Ben published *Poor Richard's Almanack*. An almanac is a book that has a calendar and tips for farming and managing the home. Ben's almanac was different from others. Using the name "Poor

Philadelphia became Ben's new home. Shown here is the State House, the seat of government in Pennsylvania.

Richard," Ben wrote funny sayings and stories. People enjoyed the almanac, and soon Ben was selling 10,000 copies a year. "Poor Richard" made Ben rich.

A year later, Ben visited Boston. His brother was sick. Ben had not seen James in 10 years, but he promised to take care of James's son if James died. When James died two years later, James's son moved in with Ben. Ben finally felt he had made up for breaking his apprenticeship with James.

Ben's Big Brain

Ben's mind worked constantly. He wanted to share ideas with scientists, philosophers, and inventors. Many of these people worked alone in separate colonies. Ben founded the American Philosophical Society in 1743. This scientific society provided a place for people to share information.

Ben started to learn about electricity and set up a workshop in his home. He was able to prove that lightning was electricity. His experiments attracted the interest of European scientists. Universities in the colonies and Europe awarded Ben college degrees for his work.

Poor Richard's Wisdom

Poor Richard's Almanack was a guide to weather forecasts, farming, and other information. Most colonists did not own many books, but almost all had a Bible and an almanac.

Ben's almanacs were well known for their witty sayings. He wrote funny stories that would continue from year to year, encouraging people to keep buying his almanac. In one year, "Richard" talked about the laziness of women. The next year, Richard's wife, "Bridget," wrote about the worthlessness of men. This tongue-in-cheek battle of the sexes went on for years. You may have heard some of these sayings from *Poor Richard's Almanack*:

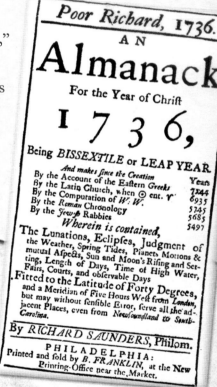

A penny saved is a penny earned.

Fish and visitors smell in three days.

Haste makes waste.

Three may keep a secret,
if two of them are dead.

Don't throw stones at your neighbors',
if your own windows are made of glass.

He that scatters thorns should not go barefoot.

"Poor Richard" Sets Sail

John Paul Jones was an American hero during the Revolutionary War. Jones commanded a colonial ship that raided British ships, taking their supplies and ammunition. Jones named his ship *Bonhomme Richard*, in honor of Ben's *Poor Richard's Almanack*. *Bonhomme Richard* is a French phrase meaning "poor Richard." In this picture, the *Bonhomme Richard* defeats a British ship named the *Serapis*.

Making Life Easier

By the time Ben began his electrical experiments, he was a successful businessman. He also filled his first public role as a Pennsylvania lawmaker. Ben wanted to serve the public, but not just as a politician.

Ben's many ideas to make life easier included helping to get Philadelphia's streets paved and lighted. He created a volunteer fire department to fight fires, which were a big problem in colonial times. He created fire insurance as a way to help people start over after a fire. He invented the Franklin stove, which was warmer and safer than an open fire. He invented bifocal glasses and the lightning rod. These are just some of the ideas that sprang from Ben's brain.

A Few Bright Ideas

Some of Ben's ideas, inventions, and improvements were:

Bifocal glasses

Paddles and flippers for swimming (his first known invention at age 16)

Electric battery

Lightning rod

Sea anchor

Franklin stove

Long-arm tool (to grab things from high places)

Volunteer fire company

Ben never applied for legal protection of his inventions. Instead, he wanted people to copy and use them.

Ben Stops the Presses

By 1748, Ben was busy with interesting experiments. He decided to leave his printing business. Ben published the *Almanack* through the 1750s, but he devoted most of his time to science. He and some colleagues figured out how to capture the power of electricity. He created a machine that gave off electricity. It was the first electrical battery.

Word of Ben's skill as a printer and scientist spread to people in the colonies and even in Europe. People admired his ideas and his willingness to work hard. They respected his opinions and wanted to know his thoughts on many subjects.

The First Library

In 1731, Ben founded America's first public library, the Library Company of Philadelphia. Members paid a yearly fee to borrow books. This library still operates.

Ben also helped start the country's first free public library, in Exeter, Massachusetts. Exeter later changed its name to Franklin in honor of Ben. The townspeople asked Ben for a bell. Instead, he sent them books, saying that those would be better for the town. The books from Ben are still in a cabinet there.

Chapter Four

A Public Servant

Ben could have lived his life performing experiments. But even while absorbed in science, he eagerly accepted various public positions.

Ben was named joint postmaster general of the colonies in 1753. He finally had the chance to connect the colonies with one mail system. He traveled many of the mail routes, created a more efficient postal system, and cut delivery time.

Ben served in Philadelphia's city government and Pennsylvania's colonial government. He continued to publish his ideas about politics.

From the late 1600s until the mid-1700s, each colony operated separately from the others. Ben believed that the colonies should unite to work better and become stronger. In 1754, Ben published the colonies' first political cartoon. It showed a rattlesnake cut into eight pieces, representing eight colonies. The words *Join, or Die* appeared beneath the snake.

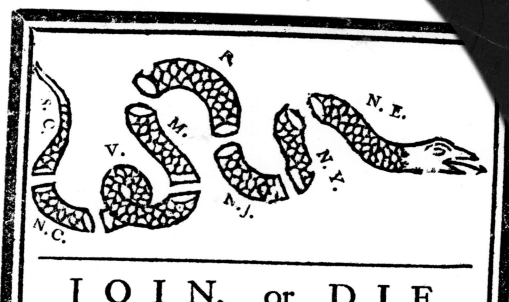

JOIN, or DIE.

Ben published his first political cartoon in the *Pennsylvania Gazette*. The cartoon showed Ben's belief that the colonies had to work together. If they did not, they would die separately.

That same year, the French and Indian War (1754–1763) raged in western Pennsylvania. Britain and France both wanted to control settlements springing up in the western part of the colonies. France encouraged some American Indian groups to attack British settlements. Suddenly, the Pennsylvania colonists needed a militia. This group of volunteers helped fight against such attacks.

By now, Ben was 50 years old. Yet he began a militia and became its colonel. He and his son William traveled the wilds for two months. They strengthened the British settlements in western Pensylvania and scouted the area.

Ben Sails

William Penn had founded Pennsylvania in 1682. The Penn family owned much of the colony's land but lived in Britain. They did not pay taxes to the colony. In 1757, the Pennsylvania government sent Ben to London to convince the Penns to pay taxes on their land.

Deborah did not want to sail with Ben. A quiet woman, she felt uncomfortable with Ben's friends. Ben and William packed and left for London.

The Penns ignored Ben as long as they could. They worried that he was becoming too powerful and might take control of Pennsylvania. Meanwhile, Ben met with many important scientists and scholars. Everyone wanted to share ideas with the famous Benjamin Franklin.

Years in London

In London, William attended law school. Ben continued his electrical experiments. Ben and Deborah exchanged many long letters full of news and love. They shipped gifts and food back and forth.

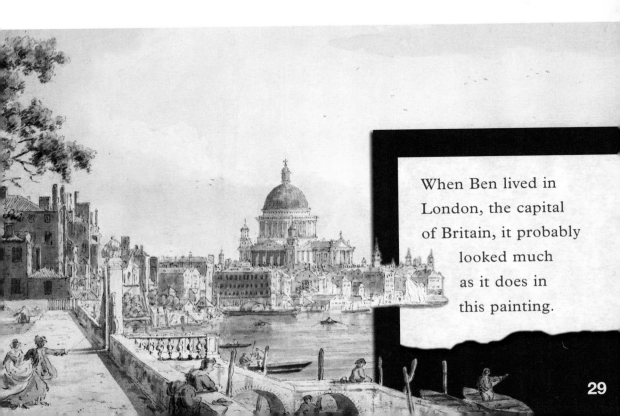

When Ben lived in London, the capital of Britain, it probably looked much as it does in this painting.

After five years, the Penns finally agreed to pay taxes to Pennsylvania. Having completed his mission, Ben set sail with William for the colonies. By then, William had married and had been appointed the governor of New Jersey.

Ben Sails Again

In 1763, the French surrendered Canada to Britain. The long French and Indian War had been expensive. Britain needed cash, and the colonies seemed like a good place to get it. The British decided to tax the colonists to raise money. The colonists said they should not be taxed unless they could vote for the people who made decisions about taxes.

Several colonies wanted Ben to sail again for Britain to argue against the taxes. He begged Deborah to come with him, but again she refused. As Ben sailed away in 1764, he did not know he would never see her again. Arriving in Britain, Ben found that his work was cut out for him.

"The Mother of All Mischief"

Ben met with Parliament, Britain's governing body. Its two political parties were the Whigs and the Tories. Whigs were sympathetic to the colonies' concerns. Tories believed in continued British rule in America, and they held the power.

In 1765, Parliament passed the Stamp Act. This law forced colonists to buy a special stamp before getting certain documents, such as a will. Colonists even had to buy stamps for newspapers and writing paper. Ben called the act "the mother of all mischief." He was loyal to Britain and wanted the colonies to remain British. But he was afraid the act would anger the colonists, and he was right.

Ben argued against the Stamp Act. Eventually, the tax was lifted in 1766. The colonists celebrated up and down the coast, but the celebration did not last long.

Colonists had to pay for stamps like these when they bought paper goods.

Chapter Five

The Road to Independence

The Stamp Act had been struck down, but Parliament passed other heavy taxes. Ben stayed in London to argue against these taxes. Tensions between the colonies and Britain mounted.

Politics ruled Ben's time, and the days turned into months. Ben began to believe that Britain would never respect its colonies in America. He wrote biting articles that made fun of how Britain ruled its colonies. Ben's enemies in Britain began to outnumber his friends.

At home, Thomas Hutchinson, the Massachusetts governor, wrote several letters to the British government. He said that rights should be taken away from the colonists. Ben somehow received the letters. He allowed some friends to read them, and soon the information appeared in Boston newspapers. Upset, the Massachusetts colonists drove the governor from the colony.

Thomas Hutchinson, the governor of Massachusetts, believed the colonists should have fewer rights. His beliefs angered the people of Boston.

Ben admitted revealing the letters. Parliament summoned Ben and publicly scolded him. They took away his postmaster duties. The British newspapers called Ben a traitor. He was embarrassed and humiliated, but he held his tongue.

Around this time, Ben received word that Deborah had died. Ben prepared to return home, not as a loyal British citizen, but as a Patriot. Ben never again set foot in Britain.

Thomas Jefferson asked Ben for advice in writing the Declaration of Independence.

The Start of the Revolutionary War

Ben reached Philadelphia a month after battles in the Massachusetts towns of Lexington and Concord. British troops had captured weapons there, and local militiamen fought back. The battles marked the start of the Revolutionary War.

Ben wanted the colonies to gain their freedom, and he urged William to join the Patriots. To Ben's sadness, William refused.

A group of colonists quickly formed the Continental Congress to govern the newly united colonies. This group would lead the overall war effort.

By this time, Ben's health had started to fail. A trip to Canada worsened his condition. He returned to Philadelphia, where his daughter, Sarah, nursed him back to health.

The Declaration of Independence

The Continental Congress met again in the summer of 1776. They wanted to declare the colonies' independence from Britain. Ben, Thomas Jefferson, John Adams, Roger Sherman, and Robert R.

Livingston were to draft America's Declaration of Independence. Jefferson quickly wrote the first version. Ben offered support and suggested changes.

Finally, on July 4, 1776, the Continental Congress voted to accept the declaration. America was officially on the road to independence.

Ben Goes to France

The newly formed America believed that France might become an ally. Before the year was out, an aging Ben traveled again, this time to Paris. Congress wanted him to encourage France to join America's war efforts. France had not forgotten its loss to Britain in the French and Indian War and was eager to get back at its enemy.

Ben traveled by carriage to Paris. Everywhere he stopped, French people cheered him. To them, he was a down-to-earth American who wore bifocals and a fur hat. People were interested in his ideas about freedom and independence.

The French government welcomed him but would not help right away. After American troops defeated the British at Saratoga, New York, the French saw that America might win the war. They agreed to help the colonists.

The war ended in 1783, when America and Britain signed the Treaty of Paris. Ben was one of the signers.

Ben spent almost two more years in France. Finally, in 1785, Congress said Ben could come home. As he had come to France, Ben departed to cheers. He never left home again.

The citizens of Philadelphia cheered when the Declaration of Independence was read aloud.

Chapter Six

An Old Ben in a New America

In 1787, Ben represented Pennsylvania at the Constitutional Convention in Philadelphia. This meeting was for the purpose of writing a constitution that would guide the new nation. All states except Rhode Island sent delegates, or representatives. Ben, the oldest delegate at age 81, played an important role.

Ben was tired. Some days, he had to be carried to meetings in a chair. He wrote down his speeches for someone else to read because his voice was weak.

Writing the Constitution was tense work, but Ben's humor often lightened moments of disagreement. The delegates finally approved the Constitution on September 17, 1787. They approved the Bill of Rights not long after that. These documents outlined the basic laws and rights for America's government and citizens.

Monuments to Ben can be found in many places. This statue of Ben is in Philadelphia.

Ben's Final Days

Ben was elected twice to be governor of Pennsylvania. He also led an antislavery group and wrote about freedom for slaves. States could not agree to outlaw slavery, and it had not been dealt with in the Declaration of Independence or the Constitution.

After 1788, Ben retired from public life. His daughter, Sarah, and her family lived with him. He spent most of his time in bed and in pain.

Ben wrote long letters to friends and worked on his life story. When he could not write, he dictated. He read newspapers every day to stay current with the news. Still, his pain continued and his body grew even weaker. Finally, he died on April 17, 1790.

Ben was buried next to Deborah in Christ Church cemetery in Philadelphia. More than 20,000 people attended his funeral. His gravestone simply reads "Benjamin and Deborah Franklin, 1790."

Ben's Ideas Live On

Ben once wrote, "Well done is better than well said." Clearly, he "did well." Electricity powers the world. People read with bifocal glasses. Lightning rods protect buildings. People check out books from neighborhood public libraries. People lead easier lives thanks to Ben's ideas.

Perhaps his greatest gift to us is the strength of America. As a founding father, Ben assisted in the difficult birth of a nation. His contributions as a scientist, inventor, writer, philosopher, and political leader will forever influence America.

Ben and Deborah are buried together in Philadelphia. Throwing a penny on their grave is said to bring good luck.

TIMELINE

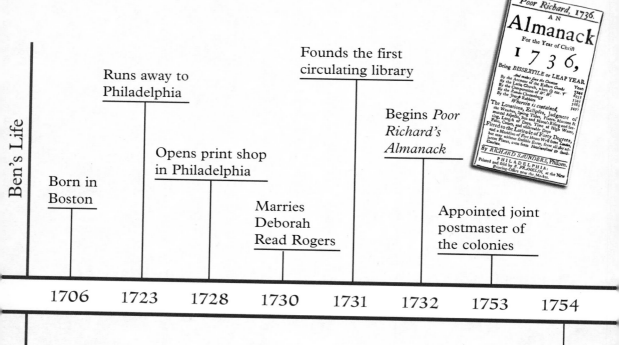

Ben's Life

Runs away to
Philadelphia

Founds the first
circulating library

Begins *Poor
Richard's
Almanack*

Opens print shop
in Philadelphia

Born in
Boston

Marries
Deborah
Read Rogers

Appointed joint
postmaster of
the colonies

| 1706 | 1723 | 1728 | 1730 | 1731 | 1732 | 1753 | 1754 |

Historical Events

French and
Indian War
(1754–1763)
begins

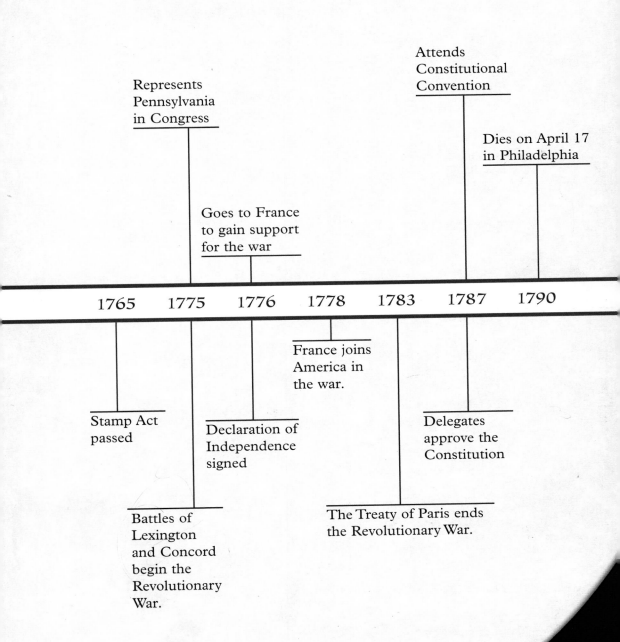

Represents
Pennsylvania
in Congress

Attends
Constitutional
Convention

Dies on April 17
in Philadelphia

Goes to France
to gain support
for the war

| 1765 | 1775 | 1776 | 1778 | 1783 | 1787 | 1790 |

France joins
America in
the war.

Stamp Act
passed

Declaration of
Independence
signed

Delegates
approve the
Constitution

Battles of
Lexington
and Concord
begin the
Revolutionary
War.

The Treaty of Paris ends
the Revolutionary War.

Glossary

apprentice (uh-PREN-tiss)—a young person who lives with and learns a skill from someone who already has the skill

colony (KOL-uh-nee)—an area of land and water settled and governed by a distant country

founding father (FOUN-ding FAH-thur)—one of a handful of men who were important in helping the colonies become one country

Loyalist (LOI-uh-list)—a person who supported British rule in the American colonies

militia (muh-LISH-uh)—a group of civilians who form an army during emergencies

negotiate (ni-GOH-shee-ate)—to discuss an issue with someone who does not hold the same view so that an agreement can be made

Parliament (PAR-luh-muhnt)—the governing body that makes the laws in Britain

Patriot (PAY-tree-uht)—a person who believed the American colonies should be free of British rule

Tory (TOR-ee)—a person who sided with Britain during the Revolutionary War

West Indies (WEST IN-deez)—a group of islands that lie in waters south of present-day Florida

Whig (WIG)—a person who sided with the American colonies' fight for freedom from Britain

For Further Reading

Day, Nancy. *Your Travel Guide to Colonial America.* Passport to History. Minneapolis: Runestone Press, 2001.

Giblin, James Cross. *The Amazing Life of Benjamin Franklin.* New York: Scholastic, 2000.

Heiligman, Deborah. *The Mysterious Ocean Highway: Benjamin Franklin and the Gulf Stream.* Austin, Texas: Raintree Steck-Vaughn, 1999.

King, David C. *Colonial Days: Discover the Past with Fun Projects, Games, Activities, and Recipes.* American Kids in History. New York: J. Wiley and Sons, 1998.

O'Hara, Megan, editor. *A Colonial Quaker Girl: The Diary of Sally Wister 1777–1778.* Diaries, Letters, and Memoirs. Mankato, Minn.: Blue Earth Books, 2000.

Todd, Anne. *The Revolutionary War.* America Goes to War. Mankato, Minn.: Capstone Books, 2001.

Places of Interest

American Philosophical Society and Library
Independence Mall East
105 South Fifth Street
Philadelphia, PA 19106
www.amphilsoc.org
Scientific group founded by Ben

Christ Church Burial Ground
Gated grave off Arch Street
Philadelphia, Pennsylvania
Burial Place of Ben and Deborah

Franklin Institute Science Museum
222 North 20th Street
Philadelphia, PA 19103
www.fi.edu
Extensive exhibits, displays, and the Franklin National Memorial

Franklin Statue
School Street
Boston, Massachusetts
Former site of Boston Latin (Grammar) School, Ben's original school

Independence National Park Area
National Park Service
313 Walnut Street
Philadelphia, PA 19106
Revolutionary War and Declaration of Independence sites, including Ben's Philadelphia home and nearby properties

The Library Company of Philadelphia
1314 Locust Street
Philadelphia, PA 19107-5698
America's first circulating library, founded by Ben; people can still buy an annual share and become a member.

Old Granary Burial Ground
Next to the Park Street Church
One Park Street
Boston, Massachusetts 02108
Graves of Ben's parents, Josiah and Abiah Franklin

Yale University Sterling Memorial Library
120 High Street
New Haven, CT 06520
Home of the papers of Benjamin Franklin

Internet Sites

Bryn Mawr Virtual Tour Through Historic Philadelphia
http://www.brynmawr.edu/iconog/Kids/intro.html
A virtual walk through the Philadelphia of Ben's time

The Electric Ben Franklin
http://www.ushistory.org/franklin
Information and links on many subjects related to Ben, his life, and his time

The Franklin Institute Online
Benjamin Franklin: Glimpses of the Man
http://sln.fi.edu/franklin
Easy-to-understand information and activities for students

The Library Company of Philadelphia
"At the instance of Benjamin Franklin"
http://www.librarycompany.org/Instancedefault.htm
A history of Ben's first library

Thinkquest
An Enlightened American
http://library.thinkquest.org/22254
Franklin information for teachers and students

Thinkquest
The Revolutionary War: A Journey Towards Freedom
http://library.thinkquest.org/10966
Revolutionary War information and games for teachers and students

Index